HAPPY HEALTHKINS

by Jane Belk Moncure
illustrated by Lois Axeman

THE CHILD'S WORLD
ELGIN, ILLINOIS 60120

Distributed by Childrens Press, 1224 West Van Buren Street, Chicago, Illinois 60607.

Library of Congress Cataloging in Publication Data

Moncure, Jane Belk.
   Happy Healthkins.

   Summary: Healthkins explain some ways to stay happy and healthy: sharing, playing fairly, taking turns, and talking about problems.
   1. Emotions—Juvenile literature. 2. Conduct of life—Juvenile literature. [1. Behavior. 2. Conduct of life] I. Axeman, Lois, ill. II. Title.
BF561.M65   1982   158'.2   82-14794
ISBN 0-89565-243-9

© 1982 The Child's World, Inc.
All rights reserved. Printed in U.S.A.

1 2 3 4 5 6 7 8 9 10 11 12 R 89 88 87 86 85 84 83 82

HAPPY HEALTHKINS

Meet the Happy Healthkins! They know that staying happy helps people stay healthy.

That's why they try to be helpful and kind to each other.

They know when people
get mad or upset,
or pout,

their heads some-
times ache, or their
stomachs say, "Ouch!"

So Healthkins say, "There is a better way, a friendly way, to work things out.

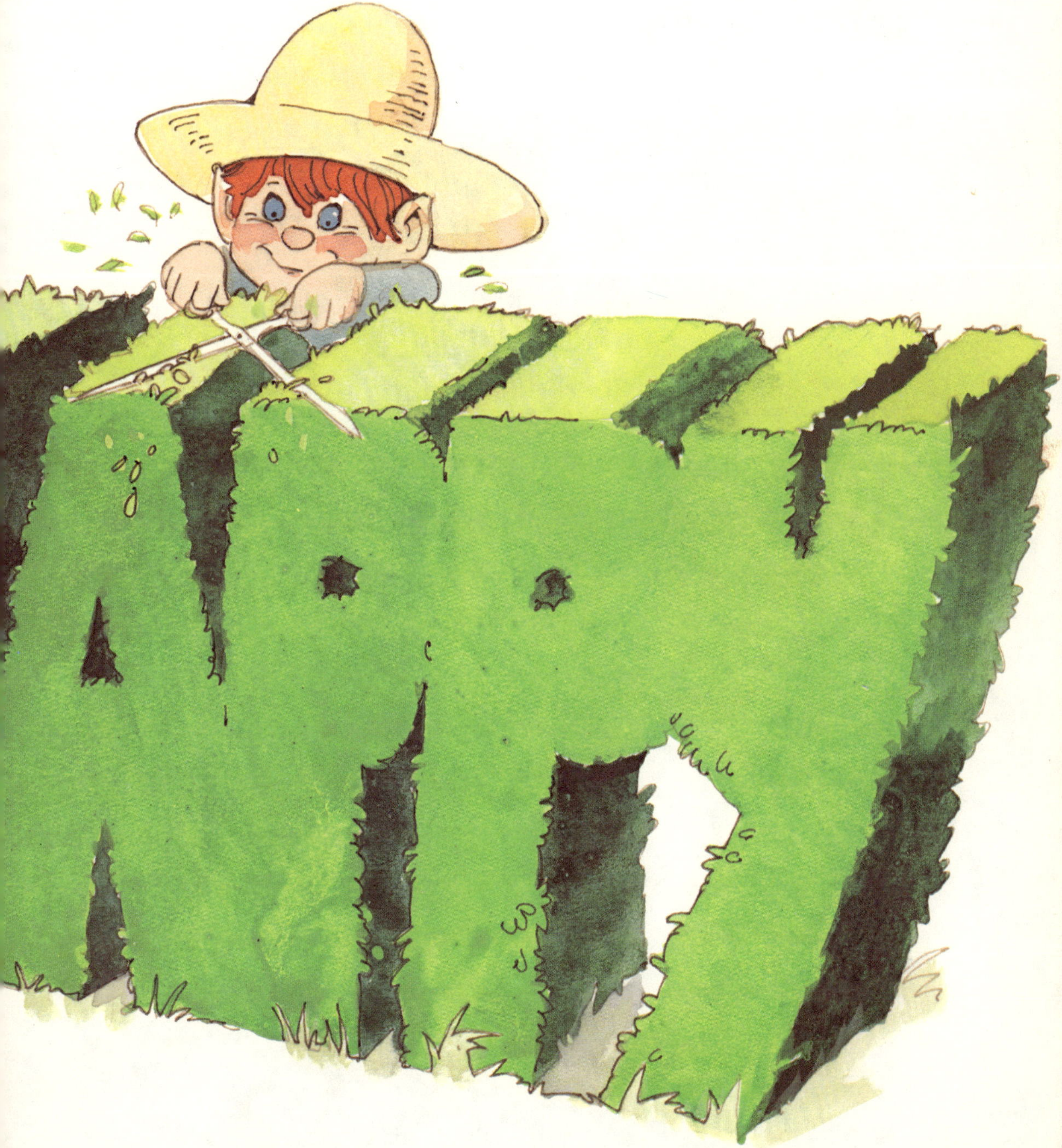

"But some people haven't learned it yet.
You can spot them right away—
any time, any day.

"We'll meet them right now,
if you'll take a seat.

"Come on; fly with us.
We have people to meet!"

"Look down below.
Look down at—oh no!"

PINCH-PUNCHERS
fight when they get mad!

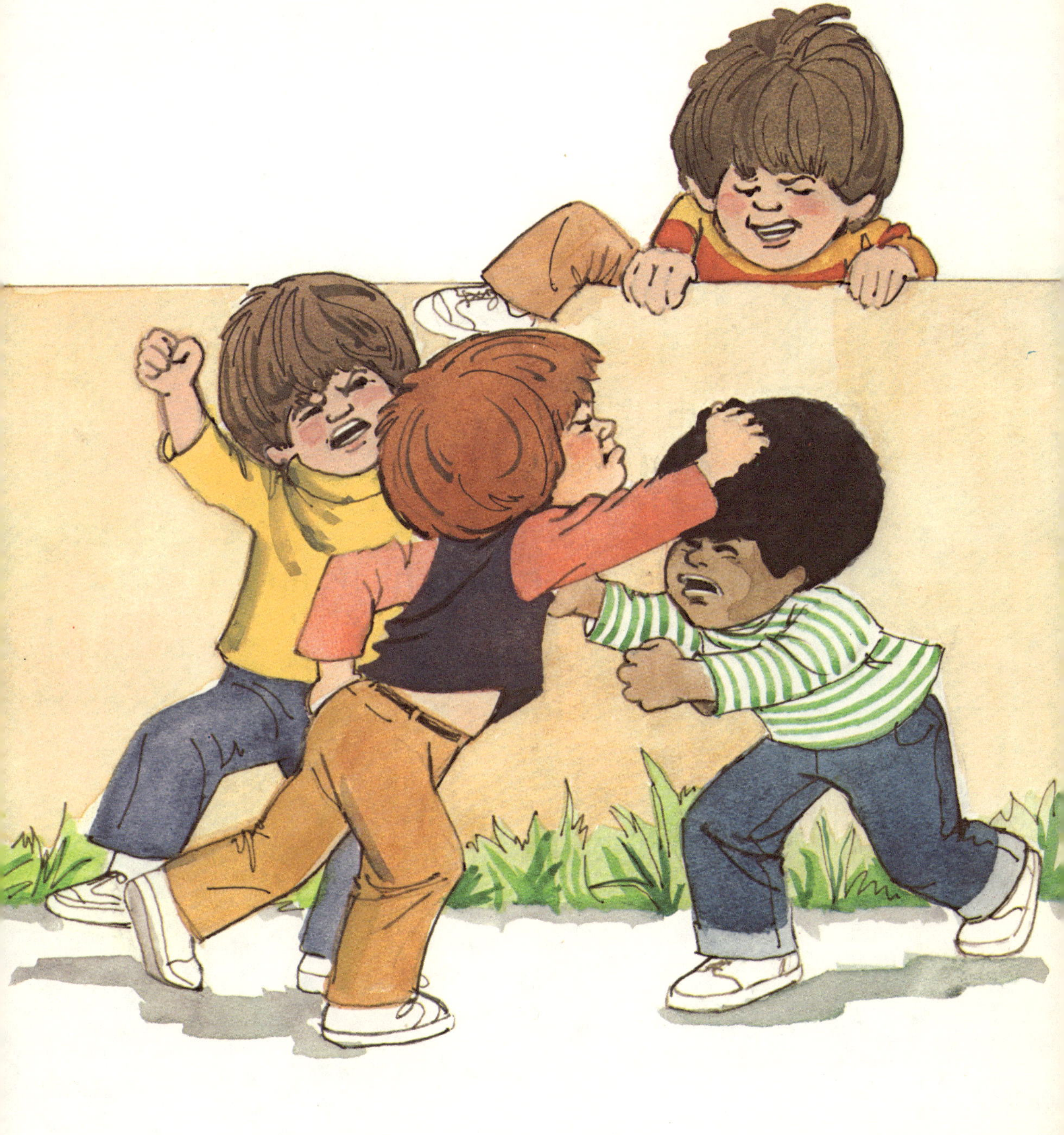

They are hit-it-outers!

Healthkins get mad too, but they talk instead of hit!

That's because Healthkins are TALK-IT-OUTERS.

"It's the Healthkin way!" they say.

"Watch out! On
my right is a
GIMME!"

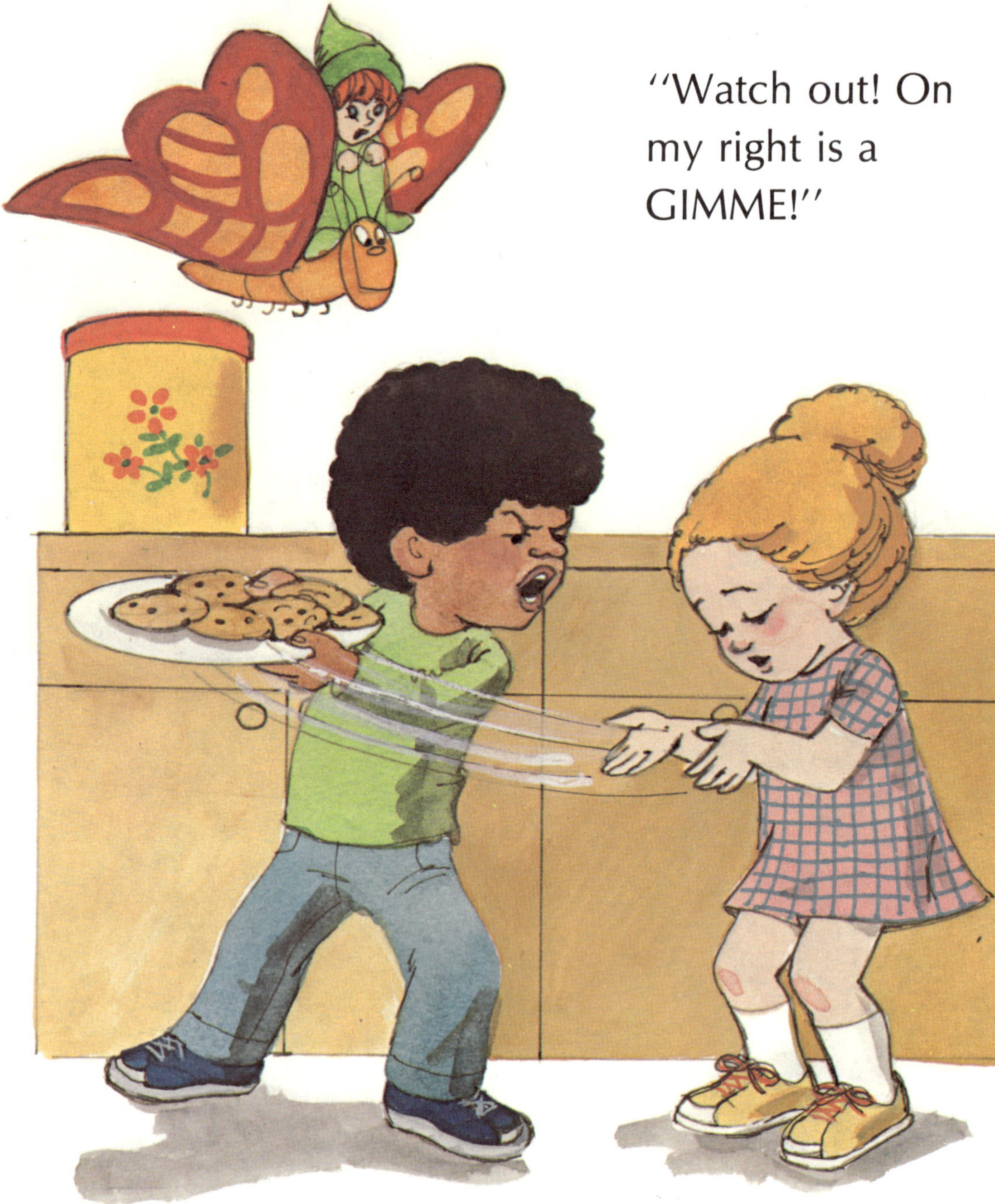

Gimmes cry, "Gimme that! It's all mine!"
Gimmes are crabby grabbers.

Healthkins say,
"One for you...

and one for me!"

Healthkins are SHARERS and PLAY-FAIRERS.

"Look on the left.
A BLAMER below!"

When a blamer breaks something, she says,

"It was not my fault! She did it!"

Blamers are finger-pointers.

A Healthkin says,
"It was my fault.
I'm sorry. I'll fix it!"

Healthkins are
MAKE-IT-RIGHTERS.

WE FIX
FEELINGS
TOO!

"That's the Healthkin way!" they say.

ME-FIRSTERS
shout and scream,

"Me first on the swing!

Me first on the slide!"

But Healthkins are TURN-TAKERS.
"That's the Healthkin way," they say.

"There's a group of GRUMPIES!"

GRUMPIES have "nobody-likes-us" frowns on their faces.

Grumpies are grumblers. They never have fun. They don't like *anything*—or anyone.

Healthkins have
"we-like-you-we-care"
smiles on their faces.

Healthkins are FRIEND-MAKERS.
They turn frowns upside-down
because . . .

. . . that's the Healthkin way!

But it's nice to know that a . . .

PINCH-PUNCHER,

GIMME,

BLAMER,

ME-FIRSTER,

or a
GRUMPIE—

can grow into a . . .

TALK-IT-OUTER,

SHARER,
PLAY-FAIRER,

MAKE-IT-RIGHTER,

TURN-TAKER,

or a
FRIEND-MAKER!

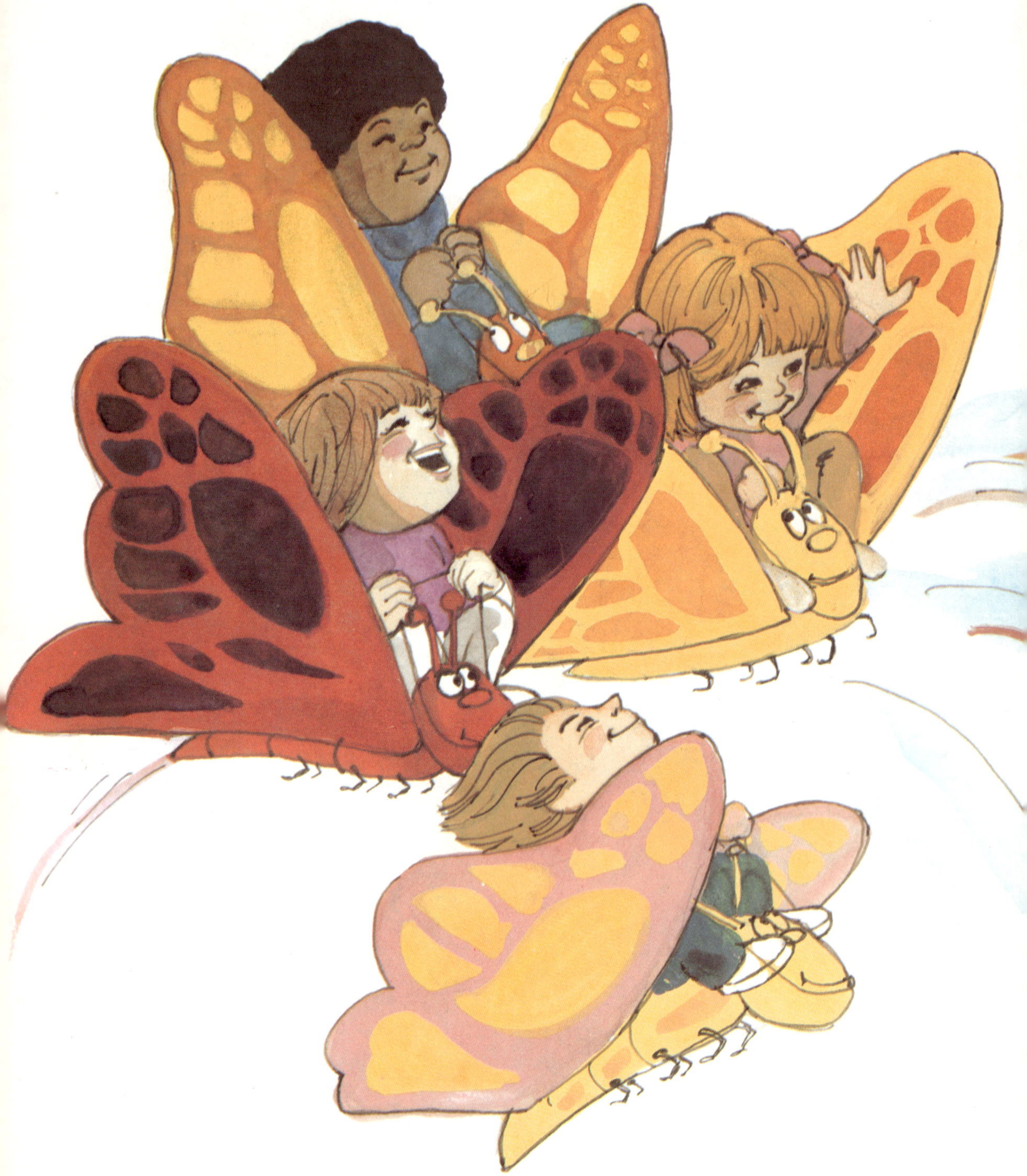

It just takes a little time to learn to fly . . .

. . . the Healthkin way!